Brightness Falls

Brightness Falls

Poems by Ellen Steinbaum

CW Books

For Kristie —
with thanks and hopes
for brightness to fall
always into your plays —

Ellen Steinbaum

Published by CW Books
P.O. Box 541106
Cincinnati, OH 45254-1106

ISBN: 9781625490421
LCCN: 2013947770

Poetry Editor: Kevin Walzer
Business Editor: Lori Jareo

Visit us on the web at www.readcwbooks.com

for Jim

We must be willing to get rid of the life we had planned so as to have the life that is waiting for us.

—Joseph Campbell

our lives have minds of their own.

—Linda Pastan

Acknowledgments

Grateful acknowledgment is made to the editors of the following publications, in which some of these poems have appeared or will appear: *CHEST, Innisfree Poetry Journal, Muddy River Poetry Review, Off the Coast, Kalliope, The Widows' Handbook*.

Special thanks for the gifts of time and space from the Virginia Center for the Creative Arts, good advice from the Every Other Thursday Poets and Sisters in Art, impeccable copyediting from Judith Redlener, photo expertise from Joshua Dalsimer, general nourishment of spirit from Meg Russell and Deborah Baker and treasured others, manuscript magic from Martha Carlson-Bradley, and delightful contributions of all kinds from Edith Pearlman.

Contents

I. Begin Again

untethered......15
begin again......16
Before I Met Him......17
widow's walk......18
Valentina Tereshkova Turns 70......19
Brave Heart......20
The Secret Life of Wallets......21
Three Fundamental Conditions for
    Happiness......22
How to Bear It......23
Adele at 100......24

II. What Can Burn

Investing......27
who would ask for this......28
what can burn......30
Acadia Summer Rental......32
Persephone's Daughter......33
Proceeding with Caution......34
Outward Bound in Belize......35
Aubade: Cambridge Monday......36
Some Assembly Required......37
Visitation......38
In Anne's Studio......39
What I Know of You......40
there will be worse (1)......41
Last night his late wife......42
there will be worse (2)......43
Getting the Picture......44

III Commonplace

Passing through Piermont......47
Shopping at Bread and Circus after Hearing
    a Poet Read Poems about her Trip into the
    Low Impact Wilderness......48
Reunion......50
On the Wire......51
how it often goes......52

cat's cradle..53
Now, two years later............................54
Losers..55
How it will be now...............................56
Going Down to Darkness 57
Why There Are Rarely Right Wing
    Poems..58
color field poem....................................59
Commonplace.......................................60
The Traviatas...61
Mapparium..62
Who We Are Now..................................63

IV. A Hundred Forevers

Thursday, February, New England.................67
This is the poem I will not show him............68
Old Growth 69
there will be worse (3).....................................70
the rose from Beauty and the Beast...............71
On the day we went to Newfane.....................72
Brightness Falls..73
stone stone chicken bone................................74
The Meaning of Poems....................................75
Heart Suite...76
Sometimes September.....................................78
A Hundred Forevers..79
Birthday for Jim...80

Notes...83

I
Begin Again

untethered

there were walls
a sofa
kitchen chairs
rumpled newspapers beneath
the shelter of the ceiling

there was time
spread slowly
the smell of coffee
solace of
pillows

now that sky and ground
are open
endless as the night
I can find
no room

begin again

a bolt of patterned
cloth flung out along
the stretch of sand

a scape of circles
each one carved by wind
deeper deeper

circle and circle
with beach grass blade
for compass

lesson that wrote itself
a hundred times
under moon

while the beach
lay dreaming
of its smoothness

Before I Met Him

I was fine
gave dinner parties
grew a garden
read the papers
paid my bills
repainted rooms and
bought new dishes
went to ballets
wrote my will
had a new book out
visited family
tried new recipes
tried new wines
made new friends and
wrote new poems
had (small) adventures
I was fine
I was fine
had (small) adventures
wrote new poems
made new friends and
tried new wines
tried new recipes
visited family
had a new book out
wrote my will
went to ballets
bought new dishes
repainted rooms and
paid my bills
grew a garden
gave dinner parties
I was fine
I was fine

widow's walk

she didn't want to
want again
yearn for arms
around her
arms holding her
new kisses
skin warmed
by new hands

she didn't want to dance
drop dizzily
from brightness
to deep shadow
wanted to go instead
on her even way
stay small and
folded from the light
never venture
into crowded streets

she never wanted
she never
dreamed

Valentina Tereshkova Turns 70

The first woman in space said going to
Mars had been a life-long dream: "I am
ready to fly there and never come back."

most of all the darkness
no tiring light
no endless looking up
just the rising out
away from solid   small

ah the weight of the world
they sigh in their tea or
nod over their papers
how the weight falls away
they say

they can never know
how the weight
rides beside you
a coat hanging
patient in the closet

how you return hard
slip your arms into
the waiting sleeves
feel the thick cloth settle
on your shoulders

Brave Heart

We know the certain circularity,
but it is February in New England,
grey and easy to lose heart.
                    One warm day
comforts us and gives us hope before
the cold descends again. Yet,
between patches of old snow
studded with newspaper shreds
and last fall's leaves,
                    this lone snowdrop
pushes up beside the front walk,
head bowed, not unexpected, yet
somehow a surprise, radiant in its
daring, in its tender risk to be here.

The Secret Life of Wallets

They seem to want to lose themselves,
get away, give us the slip, like energetic
hounds always straining at the leash. Smooth
with our constant tiring need, they wait for
the chance to slide from pockets, hide in
sofa cushions. Then the stunning re-
appearance as they drop into the lives of
our years-later selves, with expired
coupons, faded snapshots, library cards
worn to velvet at the edge, perhaps some cash.

It happens all the time, it seems—they hide
behind duct work in Eau Claire, throw
themselves into Boston Harbor, get wedged
into a tree trunk in Central Park. One fell
from a ceiling panel of the childhood
home of the childhood friend of a man
who became mayor of Tulsa.

And then, adventures done, they return
in the hands of strangers proud to bring us
the surprise and eager for our stories. We shake
our heads, marvel at these things we carried
with us, familiar as our hands, those things
we thought were ours.

Three Fundamental Conditions for Happiness

after Slavoj Zizek

first the Other
strong-backed and ready

to bear blame
for small evil, large annoyance

and then the Other Place almost
(but not quite) reachable

blinking in near distance
like a mellow star

and finally Enough
but not too much

or too predictable—minor
deprivation of a day without

coffee, gasoline, tv sets
breaking the dull habit

of assumption
the pouting wish for more

only these three things
this is what you need
all you need
despite what you
may think you need or
want, only this
despite constant
desire blossoming
like yeast, desire that
runs joy to the ground
finally overtakes it,
leaves it lying spent
and bleeding;
that turns in its bed,
restless in damp,
rumpled sheets
dreaming of
endless
hoardings; that wakes
petulant and blind
to the bright pleasure
of fresh butter on toast

How to Bear It

Try not to guard yourself,
holding rigid, lips pressed
thin, toes tight: it will not

help. Instead, pull your
shoulders down and soften
into it: all defense is an

illusion. Breathe in until
what was and what arrives
mix together, become

your new blood,
become what
you are now.

Adele at 100

thinks she may not
want to die yet after all,
after all the neat parceling
of books and paintings and
the last Nakashima chest sold
for rent and home health aides.
She thought last year would be
her last—and *good* with all that
loss and pain, discussed with
medical schools which one should
have her shell. But now she thinks
she may not want to go,
tells the tactful doctor, not yet.
She wants to see what else happens.

in memory of Adele P. Margolis 1909–2009

II

What Can Burn

Investing

risk averse
is not my
basic profile
though I have
skied cautiously
never bungee jumped or
pined to climb Everest

but I have planted beyond
zones of hardiness
tongued words even
as flames rose from them
kissed without promises
hardly looking back

who would ask for this

*We are never so defenseless against
suffering as when we love.*
—Freud

it is possible some say
to die of a broken heart
though I think too full
a heart can harm as well

> *why else this
> frazzledness tidy
> weft of days un-
> raveling in my hand
> favorite sauces curdled
> chicken roasting into
> dust while in his kitchen
> souffles float on the ceiling*

rush of adrenaline stunning
muscle leaving it helpless un-
able to contract

> *my thriving house-
> plants drop their leaves
> wither curl refuse to
> bloom his finicky hibiscus
> grazes my head fourth
> generation mimosa
> shades me like Jonah's gourd*

prey to the danger of
expanding outward out

> *but my heart beats
> unbroken now no
> recipe will save me
> bright danger pleasure
> poised for certain ambush
> no safe place anymore*

with no chance
of return

what can burn

1

measure of baysalt
pour of vinegar candle-
grease salt-amoniack
Blake called it
corroding fire
used pen brush burin
shaped each letter sharp to
brand the silken copper that
had been
before
unmarked

2

a splinter a slit
the thinnest slice
of daylight and
she
slips in
pouring through
my defended door
sliding into my skin
wearing my hair
her hunger
spreading out
across the floor

she
lights matches just
above my eyes
opens my windows
spraypaints walls
turns over every chair

now
I breathe in
the color of heat

forget the taste
of my solitary mouth

Acadia Summer Rental

I never saw the fox
though everyone else did
as it padded past the house,
disappeared into thick woods.

What I saw was lawn and
garden sloping to water,
peeling twig benches, and a
stone marker for

"Constance," "Mom," who is
"always in our hearts,"
constant as woods and water,
unlike the

faithless garden that has,
since she last saw it, required
frequent pruning back to keep
the small path open to the bay.

Persephone's Daughter

The promise matters
not the turning back
not the turning
to that old bleak space
bare and
without sun where
I bled pale
in long cold and
was lost but
see
I am here now
opening to light
offering honey-scented figs
I braid my hair
face straight ahead and
wear my name
look
you can see me
I am just beyond your shoulder
look
I am close enough to touch

Proceeding with Caution

It is never easy and only
rarely safe, so approach with
trepidation.

Creep up quietly as
if it were a sleeping dragon.
Pour drops of water

on its tail. Gauge its
reaction. Step away
from needle teeth and

possibly slashing claws then
slowly, slowly climb upon its back,
hold tightly, fly away.

Outward Bound in Belize

I step into the harness,
stand on tiptoe to be clipped to
spider wire, fly like a howler monkey
eighty feet above the jungle floor;
later climb Mayan steps unburied only
recently, drift downstream
through midnight caves
toward light.

Short months ago I lived safely
alone, put only my bones
in peril. Now with treasure
to guard, I move the chaise
to chase the changing shade,
worry at clouds he will not notice.

Inches from shore I venture
into flurries of pale fish
that swim past, middle-sized,
undistinguished as I
sputter in my mask while he,

a boat ride off, swims
with his bright school—
past gliding rays, and
dazzling angels, yellow eels,
through coral cities—secure in

weightlessness. Tethered to land,
I skirt the edge of sanctuary
shielded by umbrella, sunscreen;
watch small boats from my place
on solid sand; risk my life.

Aubade: Cambridge Monday

And this beginning is
this ending, small and passing:
the room fills with light
and music, coffee scent.
Quickly gone the heat
of you at one far edge of bed
where we lay skin on skin
all night. Each minute now
is spoken for. We slip on our
outer selves, store the rest
twinned on closet shelves. You
stroke my hair, mark me as
yours before the day
pulls us apart.

Some Assembly Required

Attraction's not the question:
we smack together like magnets
flying across the floor.
The wrenching problem is
always the one of nuts and
bolts, of fitting together
curves and bumps,
tongue and groove.
We winch ourselves in place,
part A to part B,
sanding, polishing.

Even smooth, the seam is
always there.

We lay the joists
to span our distances,
aligned and true,
brace our diverging angles
with strong beams.
We use the sturdiest of clamps,
most delicate of brads
and gently hammer home.

Visitation

I saw the wings first.
>We were in his kitchen cooking
>onion soup, a recipe we had each
>made before, alone. He was slicing
>onions. I stirred stock, tried to remember
>where he keeps the skimmer, and
I saw it, an enormous
folding in of wings,
dark grey and brown and
startling white against the
falling snow.
>Carmen had just sung
>*l'amour est un oiseau rebelle.*
>I called him to the window and
>we stood together long unmoving minutes,
>willing it to stay.
It was a red-tailed hawk, we later learned by
matching pictures—shape of head and
dangerous beak, size and color, spread of wings.
Later, too, we heard online
the call it might have made
>though it made none, only stared
>into us with animal knowing while
>we held our breath. The hawk, less
impressed, had seen our kind before, watched
for moving food then tired of us,
flew away.

In Anne's Studio

before even the first line
is drawn
is order:

each twig breathes and
each seed pod lies calm
in its deliberate space

spare, but like those Dutch
still lifes with ripe fruit, fly,
fat rabbit still furred with its quickness

and light shining down
just so on polished grapes,
draped cloth,

this, too—what the world
is made of—leaves, paper shreds, stones:
a meditation of things,

each object in its honored place
showing us what is holy in this life
is noticing

What I Know of You

Less than little:
random scenes of
aunt and mother
back stairs gossiping
between apartments,
no leftover chicken but
yes leftover soup,
olives but
not tapenade,
suede,
wisteria,
single malt,
Scorsese,
Philip Roth.

We have multiplied
our own stars,
now fill in crossword decades:
books, operas, college
roommates, summer camp,
triumphs, regrets. I know
the trips to Maine and Rome
and Stinson Beach,
pitcher of water
poured over your head,
island paradise cottage on one
long unbreathing night, and
that afternoon in Chartres
light streaming down
on stone just so, or
was that me?

there will be worse (1)

after the argument
he says there will
be worse and I
think those
are words of love

for now there are
romantic restaurants
where light is low but
we can read the menus and
wine is offered in abundance
bright afternoons canoeing
on the Charles and opera and
mornings leaning toward
each other over fragrant coffee
under the arbor with only
random hints of offness now
slight wobble flutter
lapse of thought but

yes
we are here together
yes
there will be worse

Last night his late wife

came to him in a dream
then slid away, kept
slipping out of reach
down foreign streets
while I slept beside him
in our bed where my husband,
gone more than a decade now,
calls to me from time
to time, wants help
finding his cufflinks, keys.

there will be worse (2)

there will be worse
of course
we know good is
casual and
better barely
better
but worse
is only for the
ever
for tides pulling us under
deep and fast like rip
for us running running
to throw ourselves in

Getting the Picture

1

He is my "wallpaper" now
and I am his—silly cellphone
fun to celebrate the teenagers
we've gone back to being all these years
later. Pictures come more easily than
words for this—the common terms all
seem age-inappropriate or carry too much
information—and so we cannot name
the thing, cannot say what we've become.
And so he is my wallpaper and I am his.

2

Funny how we each have
the one, the favorite look we let
be captured by the lens, same smile
or turn of head (his leans in always
toward another; my eyes tend,
inadvertently, to close).

3

The picture-taking's best within the
magic hour: just past sunrise, almost
dusk, the time when colors glow soft
gold and no flash is required and
shadows stretch deep with backstory
too tender to be touched. Sunlight
is paler, less intense, over-exposure
unlikely. Texture and shape are
what count now, but know this: it will
not last. Best not to hesitate. Hurry.
Don't waste the time before
the light runs out.

III

Commonplace

Passing through Piermont

Parking spaces are hard to find now
the town's so fashionable, but I am lucky,
cross the street and see them sitting
on a sidewalk bench, two men more than
middle-aged, eating bananas. "What happened?"
one asks as I limp by with my Velcro'd boot.
"Stupidity," I say, shrug my shoulders. "Tell us
the story," he insists, and so I do, stand there on
the sidewalk, recount to strangers the wet garden deck,
the minor fall, the x-rayed toe. "And you?" I nod to
the one wearing a knee brace and he reports on surgery—
"Thank God, healing well"; the other man is "fine,
so far." We all smile. I wish them well, sit by myself
in the new cafe where the one I remember used to be.
At every table people are discussing real estate.

Shopping at Bread and Circus after Hearing a Poet Read Poems about her Trip into the Low Impact Wilderness

we glide down aisles
smiles beatific   thoughts pure
our Saabs and Volvos parked outside
bumper-stickered "free Tibet"

it is beautiful here
what waits for us
like Christmas morning
polished food in perfect pyramids
organic and serene
milk in glass bottles
from your grandmother's childhood

fish that swam smiling into the nets
or maybe directly into the cases
to plant themselves on ice
animals that ranged free and muscular
before we got hungry

we leave only money
we take only food
homeopathic remedies
and aromatherapy sheep

shelf life is short here
infant eggplants   artichokes   zucchini
reaching their destinies fast
baby spinach ripped
from its mother earth
still soft and small
like the sweetly sticky toddlers
in our shopping carts

it is convenient here
effortless to hunt and gather
signs grammatical and even the radicchio

and mesclun spelled correctly
pale restrooms with changing tables
we leave our shit where we can
secure in knowing the fruit and coffee pickers
live in cozy bungalows
and send their picker children
to progressive schools

maybe we should have shortened the days
of the miserable penned veals
instead of the gamboling ones

roaming bright meadows
with the chicken parts and lamb chops
in Bambi-esque nirvana

but it is beautiful here
in the blond wood aisles
here in the glow
of unbleached cotton
it is beautiful here
we are one with the world

Reunion

Looking back, we love ourselves,
love the innocents we were in our sweet pageboys
and yearbook smiles, trusting in good grades
and sports trophies to protect us as we set out
into a decade too new to recognize.

God, how innocent we were, the desperate
coolness shining from our eyes and our
crisp clothes, we editors, the Leader Corps,
the twirlers and the band, the Hi-Y,
stage crew, projectioneers, the student
council members grave with their
responsibilities, and teams of every kind
bursting with heroes.

And did America get all those future nurses,
teachers, homemakers, psychologists, those
engineers? And did our alma mater glorious
leave memories to grow on? For all our trying,
we didn't know that what would get us
here was so much dumb luck and choices
we almost didn't notice making at the time.

No one is unscathed, yet here we are,
triumphant with survival and eked out
accomplishments, humbled by our dreams
and by the years that bring us back. Even
the ones who aren't here are here.

We're all here, all of us. We rush to tell
and to show pictures. Good for us. Good
for those lovely innocents, those beautiful,
serious children.

Old, dear selves, we love
you. And each other.
And our lucky lives.

On the Wire

It was just after seven,
people rushing to their jobs
then suddenly the shouts, the
pointing, looking up and
there he was
a hundred ten stories in the air,
a quarter mile straight up, the towers
not yet finished.

The night before, the Grateful Dead
had played Roosevelt Stadium—
started with Bertha, on to Sugar Magnolia, U.S. Blues;
the Astros beat the Braves six-four; the next day
Nixon would resign,
but this

was morning
August seventh
a Wednesday,
and here it was just
the wire—narrow, high—
and thousands watching
as he danced like light between
the solid towers.

He was arrested, sentenced to
make magic in Central Park. Later
he went back, signed his name high on a beam.

The president would helicopter from the lawn
in just a day or two, head back to California, jowled and
grim; Faye Dunaway got married to someone from the
J. Geils Band, the new prime minister of Iceland was
sworn in, all that same Wednesday, and then
nearly three decades passed, almost ten thousand days.

It was in the morning that day, too.

how it often goes

one
likes his fruit
brutally cold and
slightly
shocking to the teeth while
the other
prefers sunwarmed ripeness
apricots thickened
to a perfumed weight
on the tongue

with time
they learn to pull back
from the gaping chasm at their feet
without a glance
while discussing
the ideal temperature
for fruit

cat's cradle

tiny circus act:
a thin string tied tight
to encircle our
eager fingerings

slipped from hand to hand
blinked from shape to shape
tying us in knots
then unraveling
like Penelope's
never-woven web

simple stars at first
daring more and more
whirling Catherine wheels

intertwining we
lace together or
wrestle hand to hand
but we steadily
go on weaving this
meager length of line
until we are done

Now, two years later

in the warmth of our kitchen,
we retell the first-date gaffes, how
we almost didn't meet,
would never have known.

Lovers always love
to tell themselves their story,
missteps and near-misses
with forever as their favorite word,
as when Otello tells Desdemona
how joy has overwhelmed him and
how his love will live,

just as the music begins,
uneasily, to tremble.

Losers

The silver earring's gone,
the dangly beaded one I've
lost and found and lost and
found for decades—gone for
good this time, I think, the
other permanently unpaired.
I bought them near where
we skied with the children when
they still were children—grown
now, moved away. Friends, too, are
taking off, set upon by whispered ills,
diminishments, and varying decay.
One has a small apartment now,
her bed behind a screen.

How it will be now

Some people,
boarding a plane in snow,
wear the summer clothes
of their destination
while others cannot
imagine they will
disembark into heat.

This is how we are:
our next minutes
come and we
stand
in mute surprise,
cannot imagine
next and next.

This is what
will be from
here on out:
departures
outnumbering arrivals,
each unenvisioned minute
will melt into water
dry into air
leave no trace.

Going Down to Darkness

There would have been terror,
ritual chants and pleading for
their lives. They would have tried
every desperate magic
to keep the world from ending
as the animals grew still
around them and darkness
blotted out their light.

Now, in the house we rented
from the rocket engineer, we
set alarm clocks, get out his
binoculars to watch the shadow
move across the moon as we
stand still as stones,
as light ebbs away once more.

Why There Are Rarely Right Wing Poems

"I write anti-war poems," he
tells me, and I wonder who
writes the ones *for* war—
for the maiming and the glorious
dying, the planning in cool offices
with maps and felt-tip pens;

or maybe verse
that sings of ice walls
falling sheer into the sea,
polar bears swimming
ever farther, thin safety
breaking up beneath them;
words breaking down everywhere
with no smooth edge;

stanzas of captives
waiting out the years out of
our sight, away from scales and
blindfolds, sick unlucky poor,
and all the flooded shining streets
lying fallow, still.

color field poem

field of color meadow color pasture
color stalks of yellow corn wheat
honey straw banana sunlight topaz
lemon saffron eggyolk butter chrome
marigold goldenrod process yellow
Yellowstone yellow streak yellow
pages schoolbus yellow yellowcake
chrysanthemum daffodil electric yellow
and blue electric blue and deeper blue midnight royal sapphire
navy and marine turquoise dark blue and powder baby robins
egg cerulean sad song blue song cool jazz blue moon Monday
lowdown funky baby blues and black and blue and Prussian blue
lapis cyan Alice blue and blue and gray red white and blue and azure
denim cornflower indigo cobalt blue night sky morning sky shining
down lighting up color field meadow lea pasture color meadow field
field of color field of yellow yellow yellow
and of blue blue blue

Commonplace

convictions are more dangerous
than lies three things in human life
are important the first is to be kind
the second is to be kind clarity
turns out to be an invisible form of
sadness the third is to live alone
in the bee-loud glade be kind
two cups one pint two pints one
quart there is nothing so whole as
a broken heart the book of events
is always open in the middle
freedom's just another word
for Lancaster York Tudor Stuart
Hanover nothing left to lose
form a more perfect union
establish justice three point
one four one five nine
insure domestic tranquility
provide for the common defense
Genesis Exodus Leviticus
you must do the thing
promote the general welfare
you think you cannot do
Numbers Deuteronomy
let be be finale of seem
the land that never has
been yet and yet must be
Huron Ontario Michigan
Erie Superior
nothing worth knowing
can be taught
everything that deceives
may be said to enchant
everything has been
thought of before from
the very beginning
Clotho spins Lachesis
measures Atropos cuts
nothing at all has lasted

The Traviatas

In the third act, Alfredo finally
gets it, returns to Violetta,
coughing in her bed, wishing for
death, but still she sings on bravely
while we sit in the dark.

What's wrong with him, off
gallivanting in his disbelief while she's
alone and sorrowing so nobly even
Giorgio comes around, decides she
isn't so bad after all? Easy for him
to say now that she's so weak she has
only one aria left in her. Too little
too late,

all of you—Alfredo, Rodolfo, the
feckless Pinkerton. The heroines,
like tight-faced wives of faithless
politicians, drop like flies and the
audience files out, snuffling and
happy, sated with the suffering,
leaving the chastened hero to try
to love more honorably next time.

Mapparium

*At the Mary Baker Eddy Library for
the Betterment of Humanity*

Yugoslavia is not "former" here.
Tanganyika, Trans-Jordan,
Anglo-Ethiopian Sudan are
busy in their borders, Siam,
the Malay States, Baluchistan, and
Transcaucasia real as 1934. This
is what the world was. You
can walk through its heart
on a path of glass.

Who We Are Now

Waiting in the boarding lounge
for the flight that's overbooked and
somehow now without a pilot,
he decides a snack is needed
since who knows when he will be home,
asks the woman in the next seat would
she watch his bag but she says no
says no says you might be a terrorist.

IV

A Hundred Forevers

Thursday, February, New England

There was sometimes casual enchantment
and once in a while a quest.
—Edith Pearlman

It has snowed more than
seems possible, a mound on
the patio table you could sink a
yardstick into, sidewalks
glinting menacingly, hilled
outlines of cars, but yesterday
for just a few minutes the air
was dotted swiss, fat flakes
floating slowly, catching sunshine
as they fell like lighted air
onto the patio table where
with any luck we will have
breakfast again next summer.

This is the poem I will not show him

though he is an eager reader,
wants to love my words and is
quick with knowing comments, but

this is the poem about how
when we are cooking side by side
and rain is beating loud on the windows,
we turn the music up, or

how he laughs and pulls me to him,
talks to me in couple code, or turns the heat
up higher than he wants because
he knows I'm always cold, and how,

on one St. John morning, I saw him up early
in his robe, sprinkling sugar on the window ledge
so I could wake to see a row of bright bananaquits
feast in front of me before they flew away.

Old Growth

The clump of river birches went
suddenly of old age after
a lifetime of resisting
leaf blight, scale, and sawfly.

Next the hostas, bereft
of shade, suffered, scorched,
leaves wan and drooped
like liver-spotted hands.

No choice but dig those
old friends out, move on and
make new plans, thumb
through the catalogs for

full-sun possibilities—ageratum,
yarrow, bee-balm, try this,
try that and guess which ones
might thrive. Prune back, it's check

and counter-check: no blossom comes
without a bill for payment due:
coreopsis, snow-in-summer,
maybe astilbe, maybe Russian sage.

there will be worse (3)

there will be worse
we promise reveling
pitying those who
wait for perfect fruit
unblemished blossoms
we will grab the scarred
the withering
with both hands
press the sweet shreds
to our lips savor
the drops of honey
we who know
there will be worse

the rose from Beauty and the Beast

like the rose from the movie Beauty and the Beast
I tell him but he has not seen Beauty and the Beast,
not seen that rose under glass marking the time when,
if the Beast finds true love, he can become a handsome
prince again, that rose with petals slowly slowly
dropping away, the last one hanging on impossibly long
but he has not seen this; he has only gone into the garden,
cut one huge and perfect rose, full blown, now two
weeks old at least, in the vase on my nightstand where
I have not even remembered to change the water, but
the rose is, beyond all expectation, still open, full, with
every petal stretched out and not one yet dropping,
drooping, browning at an edge, or showing any other
sign of coming to an end

On the day we went to Newfane

We checked in, then hiked
up the hill and past the cemetery,
read the thin stones' names,
dates measured down to days, then
we went back to our room and he
said he'd like us to get married
and I said okay and then we went outside,
sat on the green that looked as if
a child had drawn it and buses arrived,
right there between the county courthouse
and the church, spilled out troupes of
Morris dancers, each troupe in its own colors,
with its own drummers, fiddlers, players of
accordions, recorders, some wearing bells strapped
on above their sturdy shoes, others waving
handkerchiefs or smacking sticks, all of them
dancing earnestly until they got back on the buses,
took off for the next town, and we went upstairs,
got dressed for dinner.

Brightness Falls

When the Red Line train
rises out of the tunnel just past
Kendall Square station,
crosses the Longfellow Bridge,
sunlight glinting off the
Charles and the hammered gold
State House dome, a few riders
look up, notice, the way
          in "The Hour
of Cowdust," the painting, small, un-
finished, easy to miss along the Museum
of Fine Arts corridor on the way to
Special Exhibitions in Islamic Arts,
the procession down from the Punjab Hills
brings blue-washed cows back
to their calves and tired herders
to their wives in peaceful winding-down,
late sun catching each mote to fill the air
with languid radiance in what is
sometimes called grace.

stone stone chicken bone

1

marking the house our own,
we left a stone in every room;
left, too, on a kitchen shelf
the wishbone remnant
of a meal when we had nothing
more to want

2

these totems:

want

one

when

what

wonder

once

us

3

our forever
floats overhead

even on its small string
windfall enough

The Meaning of Poems

I never liked the crusts,
ate childhood sandwiches
to their brown edge,
stopped there,
left tooth-scalloped mastodon
bones on my plate. "But that's
where all the vitamins are,"
they told me. "All the vitamins
are in the crust." When I bake
bread I stir, let yeast
grow light in salted water,
knead in flour, flattening
with my palm and folding
over, over until smooth.
I shape it—braid or boule,
baguette or loaf,
bake till it taps hollow
at the bottom. I slide it,
steaming, fragrant
from the oven, realize
I've neglected once again
to put the vitamins
in the crust.

Heart Suite

i carry your heart with me(i carry it in my heart)
—E.E.Cummings

I

A heart of wisdom,
I said that day
beside the lake,
knowing even then
about the narrowing
that stood between us
patiently whispering
its own story.

Always the unseen
universe of shadows
has its demands, its
plans to hurry us along,
the tall tree circle of ifs and
thens moving in a little closer.

2

(What I want is time
and time and time and no
cutting of his sweet skin and
no slicing through his
good bones and no
hurt, no pain, and my
arms wrapping protection
around him
as if things ever
worked that way.)

3

Almost painful that
sapphire, that magenta
impatiens, morning glories

pouring out their last
into the burnished air.
No pale new shoots,
tame blossoms now but this
bright frenzied overgrowth
grabbing for our throats
and hanging on, this
wringing out of drops,
savoring of crumbs, sharp
metal taste on tongue,
this dazzling ache of
petals littering the ground.

Sometimes September

Every morning now we
count the morning glories—
twenty-three today—
that sprung up while we
were sleeping and curl
glorious in their one
day on the arbor among
waning moon-flowers,
wisteria too new this year
for bloom, and grape vines
that persist through all our
attempts to tear them out.
A rush of birds and squirrels
harvests acorns and the kousa
dogwood's dropping fruit.

Every year I forget this—how
spring's all petulance,
with cold and rain that never end
and summer's short, winter
forever, but this brightness
will open, lit colors clear
as morning glories,
with curtains blown inward
at an empty window,
with papers flying in the air
above a desk, with something
just about to happen,
with something just over.

A Hundred Forevers

He's bought the wrong ones,
asked me to take them back
and so I slide the puny

roll of 42s—those
undistinguished flags—
across the counter, ask

can I exchange this and for
just two dollars more have
a hundred forevers.

Forever—not, we know, a word
to be believed: a note held on
past breath, the Dennis beach

beyond the oyster beds where
sand blurs into fog, or the
unlikeliness of this—our

stunned contentment that
has not, as yet, eroded into
boredom, irritation, those sodden,

all-too-human states that could
unspangle our small future. But
the enormity turns doubt aside: in this quantity,

no option but belief.

Birthday for Jim

The acorns startle in their
loud dropping to the street,
pinging off the hoods of cars
and wood porch railings. And we

are at the windows, watching
as a squirrel has scaled the arbor,
swings precariously, stretching out
for grapes, taking its fill and letting

excess fall to stone. The air is full
of herb and earth, umami—fifth taste after
salty bitter sour sweet, the taste of dark,
of deep and full, of fall and hidden wine,

and now below the murmuring the wish
swims up warm and sunlit: this.

Notes

Although the title of this book is taken from "Brightness falls from the air," many literary scholars now believe that this, Thomas Nashe's most enduring line, benefitted from a typographical error which transformed it from the original and less transcendent, "Brightness falls from the hair."

In the poem, "Commonplace," the references are from Nietzsche, Henry James, Galway Kinnell, Yeats, Rabbi Menachem Mendel of Kotzk, Wislawa Szymborska, Eleanor Roosevelt, Janis Joplin, Wallace Stevens, Langston Hughes, Oscar Wilde, Plato, Goethe, and David Ferry.

About the Author

Ellen Steinbaum is the author of two previous poetry collections, *Afterwords* and *Container Gardening,* and a one-person play, *CenterPiece.* She grew up in Wilmington, Delaware, and lives in Cambridge, Massachusetts. A former literary columnist for *The Boston Globe,* she now writes a blog, *Reading and Writing and the Occasional Recipe,* which readers can find at her website, ellensteinbaum.com.

Brightness Falls

This book is set in Hoefler Text. Considered a modern classic, Hoefler Text is a contemporary serif font created for Apple Computer in 1991 by Jonathan Hoefler. Rather than being a revival of an historic typeface, Hoefler Text is an elegant blending of the best elements of 17th-century typography in a design specifically for digital use. Jonathan Hoefler was awarded the 2013 American Institute of Graphic Arts Medal, the design profession's highest honor.

CPSIA information can be obtained at www.ICGtesting.com
Printed in the USA
BVOW08s1921080913

330511BV00001B/2/P